Ripped at the Knee

CHANEL BOOKS

First Published by Chanel Books 2017

First Edition

Copyright © 2017 by John Casey Iamb

First Printing, 2017

ISBN (Ebook) 978-0-9957766-0-9
ISBN (Paperback) 978-0-9957766-2-3

iamb@ChanelBooks.com

To my Sister,
Who gave me the pen to write with.

It is still the best present I got since 1972.

Contents

Acknowledgements

I would like to acknowledge, and thank, writers
and authors, who's works have encouraged and
inspired me many times. For their selflessness
and courage in giving what and how they give to
the public world I am grateful.
I Just wanted to say that.

If I may; Yo *Bukowski*; 'a radio with guts' made
me spill the ink that became 'Stuck on Coronado
Street'.
The poem came, and I figured someone should
write an idea from the woman's point of view. I
think your own work's like an open door at a
streamline trailer restaurant in the middle of
nowhere, with it tapping against the end of a
formica countertop and the morse code of it lost
on the small ads waitress and me sitting looking
out the window with only coins and hope.

Sabrina Benaim; Living yourself out there like you
do is one of the bravest things I've ever seen.
Think how many loves you've saved, or changed
and when that's done thanks for diggin deep and
spittin the whole truth out, it's good to hear. I
think you're mighty.

Eva H.D.; for 38 Michigans that made me pay
attention to The Montreal and hit and hope.

'Toronto' came from looking for that beer; shout
if it's ever there I'd be glad of it if the weather's
warm. Lot of hurt and happiness in 38; That ain't
easy to do, and I thank you for working hard to
let the work out.
Stop for no one.

Jane S.; There is nothing you can't write. Thank
you for *Some Luck* to a guy who needed it.
For enduring Ireland and our ways and weather.
For trying, God knows it isn't easy, to understand
here, and for putting it into words.
For the book to Brittany I owe you one. And
twenty bucks for shipping. Honest I haven't
forgotten. I'm just broke at the minute.

To my Readers; No one ever seems to thank you, I
can't thank you enough. You guys are what all
writings are for.
Mine can be a double-take on the best days,
harder than most on most days. Just that
sentence will hint at what you're in for.

Everyone takes something different from any
writing, and again on a different day. For hanging
in there, My thanks.
I just put the words out. You have to live with
them. There's a country mile of difference.
You win in my book.

. . .

A note on reading Ripped

It's a fragile thing, going out into the world naked
and emotional and in hope. All artists do this.
Actors too. Lost in the perception these
unselfish, open happenings can be lost. I don't
mean to be a critic, in credit of anything I don't
own, but it's important to be helpful and fill in
some gaps to tread the way sometimes.

Ripped isn't an ordinary layout. For me it's just
the way the book came out. The poems are like
pigs on ice as my old friend RQ used to say about
his kids. They have different styles, talents if you
will.

Little Charolais runs throughout the pages of Part
I.
It can be read every-other page as one poem. Or
it can be taken in page to page as it is, laid out
amongst the other poems. Works differently each
way.
It was an extraordinary, hurtful poem for me to
read over until I hardened to it over time. Came
to me very early one morning in winter sitting
alone by a small stove waiting on dawn.

The life we lead with someone unpresent is a common living for many of us. We simply call it 'thinking of someone'. *Little Charolais* might read much as a short story. It turns many ways, goes back a long ways. Still haunts me a little to be honest. Maybe the best poems do that. I don't know.

A red door, the poem which nearly became the title, is another one that hurts me to read. There's a lot of things goes on in a man's life at the exact same stage where he thinks everything is certain and he has no idea that nothing ever is. There's that. Plus men are mostly senseless idiots in our mid twenties. So there's that too.

Maybe someday the red door will be ok with me. Maybe it will always be too much. Might paint the damn thing again, who the hell knows about these things. There are other colours in life that aren't blood red.

Forgive if you will the unintellectual, what publishers call 'style' layout please. Actually not please; do it if you can, if you can't get over it that's your own business. I don't water your plants. I just write poems when they come and what way they go on the page is their own. I try not to change it, I don't feel they belong to anyone to do that, even me the guy with the pen.

..

Had a neighbour once took me to my first day of school, Frank. Had his own way of dealing with life and from what I saw it was a pretty good way most of the time. Loved the guy.

Donkeys years later when I was taller and had about the same amount of sense as when I started school I came home on holidays from living in the States and went to see Frank with a lot on my mind.

That's the difference when you're all growned up. Stuff on your shoulders

Anyways, I got off-loading and Frank sat opposite me at his completely spotless table, smoked smokelessly, and listened while I jaundered on like I had a half idea about life and worries.

He knew I'd get to the end probably, or at worst I'd a flight back I wouldn't miss so he hung in there like an Indian chief at a pow wow listening in silence.

When I eventually shut up and asked him what he thought, he gave me the best bit of advice I ever got, but I only realised this years later. He just shrugged his shoulders and said quietly, 'It's up to you kid'.

Ripped at the Knee

John Casey Iamb

CHANEL BOOKS

I've seen the fields of white hair on my chest
Blown on beaches across retirement brown
Seen that way I look at the world
A caged ape sitting in a frown

I've put my jaw as a man does then
An aged salmon slightly open to the sea
Let agreements out as an old oak does
Watched before me on the sand, the boy me

-        *The Old Man and the Sea*

Looking back

Shopkeeper opens his doors and people come in.
They don't even think about it, it's just the place
you go to get stuff. Same with anything we've
gotten used to. Do a week's work, mow the lawn
and maybe go get a beer. Think about life and
forget it's gonna run past you just as fast as it did
the old guy you wave at driving down the street.
Hey Harry, great day. On you go. All the time in
the world.

Banking works the same. Marriage. Love.
Flipping through a magazine outside maternity.
White coats white coats white coats. Fall of a bike
and next thing you know it's what you're telling
the guy next to you walking down the same street
an old man and the kid up the block yells hi from
his horsepower. And you can take that two ways.
Come off it right here Jim. Or maybe down there
a bit I dunno. Goin like a witch on a stick.

Whole world lies to you all your life. Only thing
said near you ever really true is the first damn
statement of your life. It's a boy. That never
changes. Everything else has a maybe.

Promise to pay the bearer. Says it right there on
the tin you and everyone else in the town at some

point hand the shopkeeper and he believes it
every time it happens. You have a great day.
No one gets it'll change the second inflation hits
or war hits or you put that bit of paper in the
bank of trust and some midnight a point zero
something of an assumed withdrawal tax nibbles
at your savings like a mouse on the corner of a
cereal box while you sleep.
Lies the whole damn thing get to go.

In a dusty barn somewheres you creak open a
door and the ghosts of lies hang inside the
dankness of a forty year old automobile used to
be cherry red and in the comfort of the same
soundin creak of ass warmed leather both a ya
gave birth to the greatest lie of all foundated on
the fleeting strength of a millisecond of life's
time.
And that's the other thing, it's never been your
own time and all the time you thought you had all
the time in the whole damn world it took to this
second, this very second to realise standing
looking at the dust that never got to gather back
then cause you were goin like Dixie nothing but
the hard formed steel in front of you they don't
make no more is still the same and you owned
nothing start to end. She's gone. The battery's
gone. And all you can say is I'll be dog gone.

Yes old man. Kid up the block. Opener of doors.
Shopper of stuff, banker of trust, we own nothing
of time but the right to look back on it and
wonder.

Three blinks after your name is figured out a stranger is asking for it spelled right cause granite ain't like paper and ah jees I'm sorry mister we don't take checks. Hell god damn it to hell what's good these days anymore nothin' ain't what it used to be where the hell's my wallet till I get this thing over with.

Can't run fast enough anywheres when you're a kid and for god knows why and can't get into that shiny cherry red fast enough either or the girl neither and every promise to pay the bearer you've tucked deep in your pocket runnin past lawn mowing grown-ups in old checkered shirts and yelled at hey Mr. Smith goes to getting you up on sixty miles an hour just as quick as you can get rid of the bills it took one long summer at the grocery store to earn so one day you'd have the privilege of being the last one to spell that sweet girl's name right to a stranger who'd yell to you one single short summer later it's a great day. Shit fuck the whole damn thing look at this sidewalk all cut up to hell. Ran this thing like I was on fire when I was a boy. Flat as a lake. No kiddin Harry. Yeah.
Jesus Christ kid watch the hell where you're goin slow down.

Throw the magazine back down and smile up at the smiling nurse with not a care in the world

who tells you the whole and only truth and
wouldn't you know you're the first dad in the
whole damn world.

Smell the grass you mowed and take a kiss on the
cheek from the woman you might one day have
to live without whether you like it or not and
when you do have time to play golf you can't
figure out why you can't cause your knee only
hurts now fifty years after you fell off the bike
you'd long forgotten about that's nothing close to
the time machine it used to be lying off in the
corner of the barn like old yeller and what the
heck is this well look at that. Now I find the
damn thing.
One picture corner-up in a crate of everything
that used to matter when you and the buddy your
arm's hung 'round both never saw this day
comin. Shit fuck the whole lot of it Jesus Christ
on a bike.

You get the same kinda lump in your throat you
got when the kid you only see now on holidays
was born and leanin back on it all you figure
somewhere there must have been a life cause
your hearts broke and all you got is time and
Christ damn it not enough to get this thing goin
again all the airs outta them sidewalls. Fifteen
bucks a piece.

So a Saturday in March you sit down and try to
put it all together. Look around you for the truth

or anything but the truth and in an old shirt you
love that's torn at the bend and a pair of Levi's
you love that's ripped at the knee you set the
shutter and hang the hands that never let you
down on a belt you've never let up on that's
never let up on you and you take one last snap.

Inside all this standing like a stranger to your own
life you try to judge all that's been through the
doors with you from the get go and try to put the
truth out on paper or as best you know the truth
or could have known to be close to it best any
man can manage.
You step back and take one final shot that don't
work out neither and say you know what, to heck
with it. This is how it is and this is what happened
and I'm all done with lies.
Hell bend it I'm all done with lies. And you walk
away.

Head back up the rise to the house that needs
painted Jesus Christ not again already and if
you're lucky to the voice you love who yelled
suppers ready that time your eyes were closed in
the last strong light of the day and the tears
flowed who's gonna ask what on earth you been
doin in that old shed again Harry and you wave
back at the kid up there on his deck waving down
smilin first dad in the whole damn world. The
hell's he lookin so happy about crosses your mind
but you know stuck back in that crate is all the

reasons you need because deep in your heart you know the answer.

Undoin laces that started life somewhere's else you take one last look back at it all and the guy across the way sittin there in his brand new checked shirt and say to no one but yourself Good for you kid. Good for you not heartbroken, torn, and ripped at the goddamned knee.

Yeah yeah I'm comin.'Fore it gets cold, huh. Ain't that the truth.

...

Part I

A Life in Poems

Little Charolais

Anytime I went near her I rose early
Watched the earth move slowly in winter
Thought of her

By a small fire in the otherwise dark kitchen we
talked
Sipping coffee steam in the quietness
Easy together

Here at last the truth

all my wives

all my wives married away from me
The first because I went to America
which might have been
something to do with the distance,
Or the French guy she met before I came back.
I tell myself different things about that one.

Leslie of course I left
That's why
she might have married someone else.
I don't know.
We don't be in touch
Or rather I do
but she won't write back

about the whiskey
I left behind.
Like Lisa -
Left her behind too
though we write
even though she married away from me
Before we met.

And the girl behind the glass
of the bus shelter that day -
Demonstrative like no one was watching.
Some story she was telling her friend
about an interaction;

Some guy, or some girl.
And the hands,
the faces
Her expressions
of talk
of what happened that day.
Of our children.

And then there's Charlotte

The star rose as the earth fell
And leaning I could follow its hide and seek
Under the top of the window frame

So is this it?
her voice leaned against me

As the earth rolled a little more
And the years passed

And the first time I ever saw her, visited again

Toronto

I've been down that road on google
thought I saw your image on a bus
but swung back to see a life pass before me
in a '66 Mustang where a sign rightfully said
Stop for no one

Thoughts of beer grew like the darkness held
inside the bars of no time
and in the hustle of peanuts I spilled things
learned nothing of myself
and held off the devil in me a while

They all have it they say
Them poets and their ways
Though besides our differences
I know you, like me, forgive them

On down Queen Street and there's a Picasso wall
Strewn curves and free thoughts that silently sing
to everyone something different
Though really when you think of it
we all get a break from our day

Eastward on I travel with my mouse
hunting for you and that beer
Past the dog's bollocks and the girl on her bike
intent on not being late
or becoming part of a bus's history

Look up and see the lines now
Hoarders of conversations, Secrets, Affairs
Torn rips of parts of people
wrenched in a mindless, irreversible heartbeat
Breath-taking eclipses of touching humanities
Lines of voices that carry the power of words

East, Go East on Queen Street West
Go on the tram line and let it chase you
to the downward dog
And ride life on a Giant, Toronto.

Maybe I could love anyone.

But I didn't.

But kisses are full of seasons

Ekmen, Friesens, Ellsworths
across the waves of minutiae

And over flower tops
they come like unexpected seasons
Catch our breath
Hold our mind

They are Summer, Rain, Regrets
Powerful as a butterfly

-    (*excerpt;* **Ripples** *- JCI*)

The times I watched her unknowing came too

      Discovering how beautiful her lips were

*Or how lovely her legs crossed standing outside
a funeral*

*Behind glasses
taking me in,*

Still.

A red door

I couldn't put down what I should have put down
A memory of the insane moment when I was
asleep at the back of a truck
Or of the school trip across the road where
daffodils lived in secret
and where houses are now
I could have put myself up sometimes too
for when I turned down the married red-head
waitress who with pool cue in hand
looked up and said I don't mind
Or when I let Ireland Road in Mishawaka have
the Buick through stop signs at one-forty
The corn it's only witness and a friend in a
mustang before me
before his father passed
Though I don't think I let him down

I could have glimpsed once in the second of life
where you have everything
And I mean everything
The treasure of existence
And if I could have captured that
Looking around at the buildings and the night
that I owned
And the woman with my child coming
I could have been,
would have been

King

When I was a child and set a bird free one day
I should have been told by someone
other than the sky that was witness to my
innocence
that I'd been a part of all of this
That I had, without knowing it
held something beautiful

and like the words of memory in the future
did the right thing
and set it free

 I have a secret dream
I can only reach for like anyone now
With the woman gone and the child unborn
and the bird long since flown
With Corn ripening and houses still pushing
daffodils down
I have a one-coat red door that I'm going to paint
again when I make it
It's the little thing that stupidly reminds me
in a world where I have nothing
And I mean nothing
That someday I will

I rose to make coffee again
This one cold
   And felt the star take the chance to sneak some
                                                    more

Voices on the radio got to farming
After reminding the country of youth

And despite not wanting to I thought of children
And if they'd walk like her

                  Always a head of me

Untitled 1

And so winter came and said to me
I am here to be your destiny
The dark I bring to clothe your flaws
the linen clutch of dreams and more
that summer sells in hollowness
and autumn leaves with nothingness

The beating waters I chill for you
are to tame the yearning,
Crest and slew

Like little Charolais

a thousand words of scream

I did it in a basement in Farmington
Stood beside the huge dryer under a bare bulb
the eyes of a spider on my back
took a while.
Had to get lost in myself
Let the brush glide me
over and back
senseless,
weeping the subconscious.
I remember the colours and how they made
themselves Joined.
Beautiful colours like
you'd see on a turned fish
Or off a rook if you watched it close enough
Where all the grey came from I don't know
All grey on the left it turned out
Beautiful colours going to it
All that grey
I forget now how it ended
Four hours of dry weeping
wet tears and hopes and dreams
on the laminate board that
was a canvas idea.
But I remember the colors
Those beautiful colors
And gold.
And the depth of it.
It was a thousand silent words of scream
that was me at the time
in the basement

Yes, I said

This is it

A Beautiful thing

I love Nicole for the soul she is
For the transgressions she smiles through life,
with
I love her for her beauty beneath the quietness
that sometimes shouts laughter at the world
Always thinking .. and that look ..
I love her for her secrecy and her cunning
Albeit maybe a small part of her nature
And I love her for her words and her eloquence
I love the graveyard sketches I haven't seen
And those of the dead trees
And the thoughts I haven't heard
And the sharing she puts into the world
through friends and her adornment of them
For how she must make them feel to have her
honesty in their lives
I love the oldness of her spirit and the curves of
her youth
I love the carelessness of her when she slumps
sometimes
The cool walk she has
Her brilliant imitations of horses
The language she gives them
I love that she can do without me
Her independence
Her time alone
I love that she has strong hands and knowing
eyes

I love her perfect feet and the dances that happen
above them
I love her beautiful, incomparably beautiful face
and that it is here in the world to give hope
that not everything so beautiful can't be touched
I love the warmth of her back and the form of it
I love her acceptance of people being different
I love her encouragement that we can all do
better
even with the simple things we miss
Which she lets us sometimes find for ourselves

I love the sound of her voice when I am with her
and when I'm alone
I love that she remembers me
I love Nicole for many things, but these are only
some
I loved her from the first moment I first left her
Because that is how you know,
And it is a beautiful thing.

φ

Every January

      we'd measure each other in the daylight

*Tuck the mornings alone into their quilts for
next year*

And take on spring like it might be different

The Flip

I'd a friend once in Boston who liked fish
Good job 'cause the place stank of the things
the Chinese got up early for
so they could take their cheeks and call it sushi

Yamma yamma yamma
my mother would regurgitate back to them
across the counter
My family used to own this whole street you
know
why cany you speak good English goddammit

We own it now the man would say smiling
You silly Irish woman
Or something like that probably
but lifting the fish and putting it to her face
Flesh. Very flesh.

And the flip of the handbag
would catch me on the cheek when she opened it
Yamma yamma yamma the man would go on
Stopping only to smile and nod
beside his silent wife

No sweets for good boys in that shop

Every year letting the looks grow more and more

Like oaks I hoped

Little by little,

but strong things

One

And the Grandfather came out on the standing.
After an inspection of the structure, its joints, its
meetings, He grazed his learned palms on the
wood and with closed eyes was given the truth of
what they had made that day. The gathered
hundreds looked up to him and ignored the
evenings wind lament that night was soon to
come. Whisps of hair and flickering eyelids
against dust awaited the score of their common
wealth.
Grandfather stood and gazed at his shoes,
contemplating as Noah must have done. He
knew the weight that was upon him. But he had
little doubt of what he had witnessed. This was a
magnificent epitome of their years of learning.
This barn would outlive the horses, outlive the
men and women before it, and their grand
children, and their grandchildren. He raised his
head and signalled; One.

One thousand years.

I write, I told her.

This and that.

a good friend

I meet a woman once a year and we fuck
She's not my only fuck
there are others
But she's different.
She likes to take her coffee in a small Roberts's
mug
and it sits where she puts it after pouring,
cooling while we heat.

Somehow she enjoys it afterward
sitting on the edge of the sofa
with her see-through gown open and her legs
spread.
See doesn't listen at those times
Though her heels are still on
And she listens real good in them usually.

First time I saw her she was like that
only she was alone
across from me in a Café,
Her and a coffee on the table
that sat in silence like a good friend
Listening

Oh, she said

That's good, isn't it?

> *And looked away I suppose*
> *To wonder*
> *Or wander*
>
> *Like the star did*

I love her

I love her here
and I love her there
I love her because she's everywhere..
I love her being the silver things
that line the clouds,
That songbirds sing

I love the way she fells the leaves
come fall
And how the sleepful breathe
I love the echo of her voice at night
that rushes make
in dance delight

I love the way the snowdrops come
soft as feathers
How log fires burn
I love the ripples that horses make
their power unleashed
when all's at stake

I love the temptuous darkening nights
that still
before her lightning strikes
And deer that in the morning mist
Like ghosts
escape the bullet's blitz

I love the dark unwinding road
at night alone
when I strive for home
The smoke in rooms where humans touch
that allow us to be
what we are not much

I love the tone that stone becomes
one moment
in the setting sun,
One night there was a single star
bright by the moon;
Her.

I love the words of poêtry
and great prose
that she often be
How cold she is when marble stone
in graveyards
when I am alone

I love the colours from raven's breasts
And how their stare the world does test
How perfume has its many lives
Birth, mature, then subtly dies

I love the sands that move with time
Living through
all mankind

And Mayflies hot upon the wing
One day of life their everything

I love that when I rest at night
I see her face and all is right
And all through these times
how I am humbled, bourne
Torn to tears
My pain; Gone

I love her here
And I love her there
I love her because
She's everywhere ..

On came the earth roll again

Shaping mountains now

    The darkest shade of blue lined the outline
And I saw the room

    Alone

Blue

Under a tarpaulin
the years went by
In and out
Always the question; Why?
Nothing to reason
Nothing more to give
Waiting for anything
Just to live
Fifteen seconds of fame
No name
But creases of skin in my memory, Remain
Twenty-thousand Rupees
How it all began
Hopes
Dreams
Anything but pain

Under a tarpaulin
Blue
Years gone by
Still the question unanswered; Why?
Dying before me
No difference from hands to feet
Bought cheap, sold dear
To the heartless, uncaring, dead-inside; Meat
But I will never forget her
Her honesty of shame
I will remember her beauty
If not her name

Here was winter again

Once more conversations coming from
unspoken words

and glances

and tea

And cold mornings no one saw in the beginning

The question

I hate when mother leaves
her green tearful eyes
though her perfume lingers and chokes my throat
And when will she return
or is this another rehearsal for the end
When her red jacket is come across one day
and her shoes abound and fall
out of the closet when I seek something
and look in the oddest places

when the things she kept in cupboards
for none to see are seen by all
and faces near to not be missed
and stand and speak of knowing her
when they seldom called

and make up things

When I stand in a garden she made by hands
where blackbirds steal a living
and murders' come for bread
when I am a stoic man
or cry a child alone
where the cherry tree was pruned
and in another minute grew

When the salad makers come
and clip about the floor

the big light on the sacred heart no more
and we see the chips in marble
where mother marked her world
her heat so taken by darkened clothes
they leave me thinking, ever thinking..

Did my silence bury bodies?
My most beautiful works of art
And wonder ..

And this is the question

Will I forgive my unforgiving minute?
or choke on perfumes past
Take bread from hands I do not know
and in pretence a man
bury all the dogs and feel no different

when my father becomes his father
before he clears his throat no more
and all their shoes abound and fall from closets
when I look in the oddest places
And the robin comes and eats the bread
thrown by hands of faces he does not know
and worms become my dogs and hug my
mother's earth

When a stench of past life perfume becomes my
rehearsal end
and my shovel hands are crossed
with beads that mother wore

and make up things

When talk is though they knew them
read all the words they wrote
knew they held me in a garden where I shook
And felt them love
when all they did was run from them
when they had so much to give
Today they waved goodbye

Here she was again

unfolding years and winter quilts

Leaning in the light of a small fire
Asking
In her beauty

For little charolais

the rain

The rain the rain came tumbling down
'round and 'round and around the town
dipping in where men can't see
hanging on a branch
a tree
Clothing moths until dew falls
keeping all the sane indoors
making up for summer's sun
when smiles and happiness and guilt were none

It repents the lame
bestills the heart
It traps some thoughts
breaks things apart
No colour hue it borrows some
the brown of tiles
green moss
my bum

Denim darkens
leather squeeks
It gleams the ordinary,
Village, streets
as windows no longer hold the faces
of passers passing
my café oasis

but wiggle onward

shapes of gore
running now
more and more
like lemmings to the waiting sea
clip and clop
some know me

Looking down
to shoes that move
like watching other horses hooves
Some look up
the grimaced bound
But some still smile
Some only frown

Outside rolled the world again as the kettle
boiled

And the star dashed
And her voice quailed

> *Slowly*
> *and with gentleness*

going

..

In the time it took to make coffee

Both were gone

Porta feriti

the two favourite shirts I own joined arms today
wrapped at the elbows from the washing machine
which is a bitch of a thing to happen when you've
coffee cooling fast
but a good sign when you've met a girl of wonder

The brown one slashed applause on a day I was
super
Working on the car making muscles
and the blue one took a hit on a fence I'd been
sitting on
One of those indecision days where hesitance
won

It was a rock and roll tuesday this happened
Arms full of laundry after the kettle boiled
and the streets were empty of tourists
and a flight ticket filled most of my jeans

Days before nine I'm all over it usually
the world and its niches figured out
have its socks knocked off illiterately
and press-shirted sip ready to conquer

But the day the shirts held together was a
hurricane day
The signal long given to the wars of my life
and I wrestled with cotton and bore its stretches
out
the slave of uncontrollable events

It was the day when it was win all or loose all
the day I sent the banana joke to Sherrié dear
The day it was cold and grey and rainy
The day Ireland came back

And I stood like always a kite against the wind
with my two shirts telling me
Torn and ripped that I was

to hang in there

Leave Hemingway say Farewell

I want more from life than this
I said,

To no one

g.

Met her on a Tuesday wearing a frown and
undressed her over tremboule four children later
while she was deciding on coffee and the kids
were playing she-started-it.
Though honestly it was our first date, and putting
genes on the menu was a secret thing
I think.
It wasn't that I thought the waiter was into her
but she had this thing about eyebrows I'd later
find out and he was drastically Italian in the way
only Italians can pretend to struggle with come se
dice in English. I'd roll any dice I'd whip him I
reckoned.
That Tuesday when I met her she was weeding
and I was knocking a hammer up and down so
she thought I was. Working. On her
I'm in trouble now was all I was thinking, even
before I just missed my thumb a half hour before
she stood and planned her approach, and in
stealth asked me if I felt like pizza; Or as it
translated to me
Spending the rest of my life with her.
Of course I went with the margarita and a wine
waiting, why not. Sure.
She stunk of the sweat of birth just then. It was
an August far as I remember. Breeze blowin road
dust coming from the sea.

It was an unbelievable thing to experience
a woman asking you if you want red or
white.
Or twins.
Jesus, I thought, I'm one man for
heaven's sakes. And I'm lucky to have
two thumbs.
Red please.

Here's the crows now
And their complete unawareness of time

Judging my immortal progress

the waiting room

the leaves are all off the trees now

Browns and Yellows.

Laughing things of summer

And Nordic air encroaches

like a silence does in a waiting room

And everything hardens against it

We look at our feet like strange, interesting oddities

Hear the ticking in our heads

Think of the little things.

Outside, like faraway places

looks wonderful,

Inviting.

As with loves though

we know better

yet still we venture fourth

Against past judgement.

This time, we think

It will be different.

The wind came then and hustled the flower tops
outside

as the sky blued

       And inside I tossed the cold coals toward the
                        bright flames
To be at something

                And to listen for Glenda

time

I find myself slowly but surely saying goodbye

Chance meetings I away from
Glances down at the driveway remembering my
Godchild's hair
Wanting to look back up at her youth
Her wrongful placement at the necessity of
importance.
And yet I trudge on
To nothing important.
Time.
That's the word,
Time.
How long? I wonder
When I look at faces
And when I remember
Mammy at the fence with Margaret
And snowdrops
And lies.

Spring and all it is is here again
And it is beautiful.

And so the silence wouldn't be
Like the bright flames before I tossed the cold
coals

So all encompassing

Scuffed shoes

Something in me says stop lie down
Another thing pushes don't, keep going
there isn't time
you can't make more time
What if tomorrow when you are more tired
there is something else to do
that has to be done
and you are stuck still in today
Always today, not getting to tomorrow

And it passes like a bus
All the people on it looking at you
with the faces of you as a boy
thinking;
There's the guy who didn't
Who could have, like all of us did

Ordinary people who only wanted
Simple things

And the noise of it disappearing as you stand
there
watching through the heat haze
watching through the dust
watching tomorrow go away
in scuffed shoes

And yet other than the stove and the charolais
There was silence,

Still.

Our Silent Day

When I stand and stoic be
I am not of darkened thoughts
Or those of death
Or of regret,
Or loss
I am of sense of thoughts of love
Of warming smiles
Your hand upon my womb
I hear not people's words
Nor in their faces pass
I do not feel their warming smiles
Or in sweet nature
Any comfort find
I am, at heart, a weeping child
My world so still
My cry the wind of trees in June
Their Scream-blown seeds
my silent tears of loss
I stand alone.
I stand alone for you
and spill your tears
upon the dampened soil
I stand alone for us
On this, Our silent day
And in my silence
Without words
I say
Goodbye

On and on went the winter months

And with every morning came the hide and seek

And Glenda

Stuck on Coronado Street

Push and turn
in endlessness before the summer goes
Reaching on shaking limbs
to the back of the bed
Every year passing in a weekend
The weeds laughing at her
as the sun beat down
seeping onto her skin
exploring her as maybe a stranger would
gently about her curves
tonguing heat along the lines of a bathing suit
too far a drive from the sea-side

All she had was the heat of this
digging in the garden at the thought of it
with it pressing on her

But inside her was a beautiful thing
that yearned for him
No one in particular
but a man
any man
any man who would want her enough like this
to take her soiled
and push into her as she did the trowel
over and over unthinking

Inside the musk of the garden shed perhaps
Against the wall till it hurt good
shaking things from shelves
thumping off the jam jar to the floor
the crash of glass before the clasping silence came

Soil and its beautiful damned smell
why she had not said yes
all those years ago
before the dresses mattered too much to take to
the garden
Not good enough Mother had said
Wait
you'll see
you have all the time in the world
Time
What a con
How could she have been so cruel?

Time ..
Maybe she didn't know
Not understood
how it flies now
Years passing like houses on a bike
four, five, ten, twenty
Mother ..

Mother what were you thinking ...

Push and turn ...
I'll grow roses here
And Rhubarb
so I have something to outlive
stuck on Coronado Street
head dipped to din the noise
of people who are waiting
with all the time in the world

And the heat of this now
the heat of all these years
Push and turn
Run back
run back to it
Harder and harder
Run back and say yes, Yes
somewhere in the row of houses
where you could have stopped
Stopped and not given a damn
Pressed against a doorbell
your finger on the heated round tip
Wetness on a tight brow
His
Anyone's ..
Harder and harder
Push and turn ..
Sweat and breath and life

She was wanted once
Had known it
And now
Driving a trowel against the earth
a dot in all this madness
Push and turn
Say yes
say yes until the aching stops
until the breathing and the laughing comes
and your heart pounds on shaking limbs
as music comes oddly from the rooftop
and a man looks away

The fire would frickle now and then like a new born
Learning we would tend it

And we'd let the star rise

once more

Once more death came amongst the pigeons
In the heat of a sun in Krakow
Lost on marble and absent of thought really
I watched things remarkable

Locked in a time lock
I dispensed of the ordinary
Felt the suppressed
Calmed in me

Sitting in the shade a group of school children
passed me
One of them with the look of her and me
Turned to her friend and said
Something that might stay forever

And in the words that I didn't hear
Will never hear
Against the background of unnamed music
I said goodbye to my daughter again
I said goodbye Arianna
And I cried writing the words you left me with

Making coffee I'd get to watch her presence

Pouring

out of water

My lips and all about me are sewn
To the myth of a new life and welcomeness
The re-wombing of grown children
Into the tents of their silent mothers

Though sleep still offers respite
Its offerings are as imaginary
and as wanting as the wake times
Spent in the human humming of flies

Gone are the days and nights
The known turns of every lane and sunshade
The voices
The past
The future

Inside me grows a new girl.
A fish learning to be
Out of water

And steps away from an embrace
I'd listen as the star snuck away again

And smiled at me

Zoë

Is this really what I see?
Stars above that seem to shine on me?
A silence that's kept from year to year,
In still night air
that seems to somehow steer?

And a lawn's scent that stops a thought,
of meandering nothings
Worries of naught?
Does the chestnut bloom in resplendence of self?
or as one last show of Beauty, Wealth?

The stars I know are long since dead
And the silence of yesteryear, long since spent
The scented air is absent now
And thoughts abate
of What is?, and How?

Naught a worry, that meanders still
As the chestnut sprouts
Despite its will

What we see, we see.
What might be, might be;
Just stars
And grass
And a chestnut tree

It was a lovely game we played those mornings

Just the silence of it all

"And memories of static looks that remain
Artforms in the corridor of my life where I have
seen you."

- (*excerpt; **None more than you**, JCI)*

As I rose early
And went to her

In Winter.

. . .

Part II

Hello

When you break up there's a high
Like with any serving of freedom
Sacrifices aside.

Torn things from the track you should have quit
while you were ahead
give you time to mend
But mostly
Holding your calves at night
and finding grace etched somewhere in the carpet
There's relief

After the false smiles that soothe neighbours
And settle the dog's tummy

After the nods that thank postmen
But tell them you're no easy picking yet

After the two o clock in kitchens
Barefoot and careless of neighbours in underwear
with your real age self in the window for
company
                    You realise
Not everything on the countertop is yours

But you now own the silence outright

And after miles and miles
Of walking alone
After the relent to instant carbohydrates
The standing at gas pumps
on always cold-wind nights
that blow doubt and promise nothing

After the numb, beeping checkout queues
And after the friends have done their duty
and gone back to their linen
Lain tight with their lover
and been loose with your name
You strip bare at interviews
And wrap yourself in lies

Everyone sees the end from the beginning

Feels it tugging-out the corners of their eyes
At something said
that's no longer cool
And politeness ruled amongst the winter plateau
of the tabletop
Treed with the torsos of so-called friends
        Who brought good wine bought on sale
                (I'm almost sure now)
        leaned this way
and that
toward the light

or away from the wind of conversations

How long does it take to write a poem?

One of them usually comes round to asking

       Hand curled under her chin like a pussycat
                     Meoowwing something
that's regurgitated from inside a wine glass
and hummed to you eventually

with a stilettoed foot ticking unseen

           like an expensive tail

Sometimes half a cigarette, I'd say.

Sometimes a whole friend

Oh.
was what they always said then
after laughing
Or not

                But always raising one eyebrow
                   after everyone had the chance

to look at everything but me
sitting rubbing my tiny reflection in the glass
before I looked up straight at her
and cat stared at me like prey

                        Smiling Macavity

(There's always one who creams
under the cotton they reckon.)

Buses too, can tell you a lot of things

The disguise of mankind
wrapped inside a sardine tin
Looking distant

                                        Afraid

                        at one level or another

                        Of speaking

Its times like those you get to notice
            Things about you that need changed

Shoes
and jeans with small crotch holes
            Haircuts on the big head in the glass

Enormous stubble that needs attacked
like let-loose brush in the backyard of a rental
house
Or a relationship that needs shrugged off
like an old jacket

And put out of its misery for Goodwill

It's the cornered mouse feeling that does it

When legs stop beside you in a bus
    Or when you're on stage with the fridge door
                                         open
  and one of those make or break questions come

Or when you have to fix your finger on a word
for the first time since you met
before you look up
Measure your glasses off
And have to answer

How long your jeans last

Or where you sleep that night

Can depend on a single wrong word

Long past when things were easy
and honestly blurted like startled pigeons
from the clover patch of your mouths

Everything began the concealment
that began the end

On a sunny drive home it can hit you
Or half way to a dinner party
Talking shite because the radio would be too
obvious
Might make you turn your head

                              Or look in the rear view mirror
                                              and say

Hello

to the reason you can't see back to where you
used to be
that's sitting in the back seat
waiting for someone to say
                              Them pigeons have flown
                              And they ain't comin back

Admit it

There's three of us in this now

Looking forward

It can escape from a goodbye kiss in the garage
either
On an otherwise normal Friday morning
that held kisses longer
amongst the loyal smells of Saturdays

And masked in a revolting perfume
Dressed in red

With a forced smile of reluctance,
hint at something that will never happen again
as politeness tugs the corners of her mouth
So the chickens don't escape

I knew a man once who left his wife chopping
                                                    wood
as she waved goodbye from a white Tahoe in
                                                  mittens
                          with eggs on her mind

And the side window was still foggy
Blanking the forced upturn of the corners of her
eyes
and he found enormous interest in a half log by
his feet

It was the morning her head was set on a huge
thick scarf
And couldn't turn to look at him

It being winter and all he'd say later over beers at
The Iron Horse

And nearly two years after, he moved out
wearing the same big-squares shirt
And most of the same hair while I got the tab
Poor bastard.

Every time my lover hung up the phone to her
husband

I realised

No one in love
should ever need so many words

To say goodbye

. . .

Part III

Amelie

The poet and the fly

Once a week he goes to the flower place with the
café
and writes his own interview in the magazine he
uses
to try and not listen to
the two old ladies who are happy
about God knows what
Just being girls again like they used to be;
Only most of their friends are gone
and neither mention it.

Inside him he is dressed in Louis Vuitton
with a medallion for the laugh of it

How solitary the life of a writer

And dances in his mind to a funky awaiting
French toast
as the woman he'll name a child after cracks the
eggs
and the half-specked woman by the window-sill
frowns a laptop
Wrestling words from it like she would a
foreigner on holidays
Is it this way, or that?

All smiles. And nothing behind them.

Lies are like that, he thinks.
And all acting is lies.

Amanda breezes over with a moustache mug
Full of everything she's going to give her husband
when they marry that September

And practices asking is it hot enough
and if a man might want something else,

like her hair grasped
or his shoulder casually touched.

While it steams, Enjoy.

The flowers all seem distant now
behind the glass that marks where the stage
begins
And inside themselves people practice their lines;

Grey men's mumbles' that mask the curves of the
waitresses
dip between the designer ads in Interview,
As do the too-long stirs of the young married
man's in his coffee mug.

Though his wife knows,
men can be animals like that when food's around

But no one shoos the sly fly.

The dance ended, Jimmy Choo plays
perfect curves on the foot of an upside-down
model
April
while his scrambles come from Hannah
and all hell breaks loose;

The church bells echo with the sound of her
name again
and God signs with water
on the smallest most important thing in his life;
The Godfather epically striking at death

(though there's no cannolis here, only muffins)
Some large, Some small.

(Hannah, he's told, takes the small ones).

Amanda has a new girl too,
Folding napkins with the care of a sociology
degree
and the old woman in the perfect body of the
quiet girl
heats the cheeks of the young married man from
ten paces
While Hannah's sister draws a line with the family
beauty;
Curtains up.

Those lips of hers are really something else
he thinks; Jesus what a mouth,
And I've heard her speak
and it is immeasurably catatonic

While the whole thing started where potatoes
were

On the side of the road and he'd known no one,
there was a girl there he'd loved,
Imperceptibly,

And he'd stuff bags of turf through the dust and
the heartache
until she'd look at the hundred and say;
They're beautiful.

There's something beautiful about them.
Isn't there?

And he'd scrape the windows with a razor,
each one of them something to him
because she cared,
and he cared very much for her,

brushing her castoffs aside like love lost
on mornings when no one came

And he'd play Amelie alone,
and dance with the broom of her in his hands
to the rhyme of another Summer that never
ended

Though it was in this play already something past

Before Hannah and Claire,
and the woman he'd name a child after,
                                    there was him

                              and there was this

                                 and it was silent
                              and it was everything,

          Everything.

From the corner

and with tears inside
he watched it;

Voices and silence all at once
Amongst the nothingness
and the new everything,

Amongst the stirs in the places he'd committed to
on mid-days
when only lonely women came

and when Saturdays were coffee times
and nothing else after the window cleaning
mattered to him
only Hannah
And everything
And words

and Amelie.

The grey men and the sly fly leave the muffin watch
        and pay their prices when his toast arrives;

Sly to the blue grave

and the grey men to the hot chic
who'd hovered over table five.

(Though they should have paid the young guy's
wife for dessert.)

Not many men leave a café without paying in full.

.

And no flies

                              Or writers,

do.

...

Part IV

Come a tuesday

Come a tuesday

we see our faces everywhere
In all but the usual proper places.

Not in glasses before we drink the milk
or upside-down in spoons,
like we used to when we were kids
Which was the right way.

Yet our faces are before us everywhere,
They're glimpsed in rear-view mirrors
Look up at us from carefully carried empty plates
that once had something we cared to see.

Sips of brow lines get noticed in cups of black
coffee
And laptops
show us their stoic face in mornings
Like a passport so we know ourselves
Yes, you are me.
Still
hunters see their faces in the life-like eyes of
fallen game

Cattle the same to the abattoirist on a tuesday,
who in his sharpening gets refractions of the
killer

him.

Rarely these things are women though;

                                      They, I think kill slower
From birth we are chipped at by Mothers
Telling us to go look at our face

Wipe the filth from it.

..

Oddly

      we go on to seek a second mother
        - For our children.

      Always in the crowds we pass,
looking for that one thing
that's been taught to us Important;
      The resemblance of self.

Millions of them now,

stuck in a book.

Sheep, did you know..?
        can remember fourteen of our faces?

Maybe it's a feeding thing,
Something to do with survival.

        Maybe it's simply the count they need
        to make them sleepy,
        I don't know.
        Nor does their throat-cutter.

        But if I were him I'd ask.

Between our feet we see them in waters.
On sunny days that brown them

In lovers expressions something happens to them

              Something that must be beautiful
that we can never see in other things

Because that's when they call me 'You'.

In children's eyes they never change.
To the bartender who makes the best of them
neither.

Building bridges with colleagues, sounds come
from them,
Codes and understandings,
One word things that can make some people's
days.

Dead they even mean something to someone;
Hoarders of memories
Last touches
What could have beens'.

In life they are self-changing
Or pushed that way on purpose,

                              Presented again
                to the world like a home improvement;

Less nooks and cleaner lines,

While everyone who visits just can't get
comfortable anymore,
in the new place.
but lie and say it's lovely.

                    To your face.

People punch them
and others slap them

                    Peers envy them
                    Idiots laugh at them

Rain beats them
and wind tears them

                    Gravity weighs them
                    and insects bite them

Carpets burn them
and make-up covers them

                    Creams cool them
                    and kisses warm them

Friends know them
Potatoes grow them

                    Artists paint them
                    Galleries show them

Policemen keep them
Witnesses forget them

                    Cartoonists bend them,
                    and mothers love them

                    ..

But maybe they all look the same
to the knife sharpener

come a tuesday.

.....

Part V

Letters of a Mother

8-7-71

Dear Miss Conane,

Thank

You for your letter.

At the moment it is not
possible for me to travel to
Dublin, It maybe a month
or more before I can go.

It is reallykind of you
the way you have kept in
contact with ^me although I'm such
a useless creature for answering
letters. You may wonder why I
don't write more often the reason
is I have to travel to ....
to post any letters to you..
Please trust me & I will leave
you know when to expect me.

Catherine C.

18- 11- 70

Dear Father Cunningham,

             *Thank you for your letters
there ...... is nothing I can do only have the baby
adopted, ... I hope he will get a very good home
and .. bring happiness to some child less couple*

  *I hope ... they will bring him up well, there is one
thing he will always have and that is .. my prayers.
I say ... a ... Roasary for him every night.
................wrote to me, I had her letter this
morning, I could tear them to pieces, all she seems
to
think about are her damn inlaws, and the lies she
has to tell them about the baby. She also told
me she is not having a photograph taken of
the baby.   What do you think Father ? Do you
think I should have one?*

     *I met Fr._____ last Saturday night and
I told him everything, he said to have you know
just in case you might like to write to him about
me,his christian name is Martin. He is our Curate.*

  Thank you for all you have done fo rme.

                   Catherine C.

Bessboro
Blackrock
Co. Cork
15- 10-70

Dear Fr. Cunningham,

Thank you for
your letter just received.

Fr. Smith broke the news for me
to my sister in Dublin, she is in
..............hospital. I had a letter
from her, and she advised me to have
the baby adopted, so, if you could get
it done as soon as you possibly could
or get him into a Nursing Home until
he is adopted the easier it will be for
me to part with him. My father doesn't know
anything about the baby.

.... has holidays coming to her
so she is going home, and she will
cover up fo rme, My father thinks
I am on holidays with my
sister in Belfast.

If I could be back home again
even for a week, before _____ returns
to work, it would be a great help
to me, to help me return to normal
living again.

When you are writing again
you can address the envelope
"Miss Teresa", it is the "House"
name they gave me, when I
arrived.
  Hoping you will be able to do
something very soon, Please pray for me.
                    yours   Sincerely
                        Catherine C.

Bessboro
Blackrock
Co. Cork
6- 10 – 70

Dear Father Cunningham,

I arrived here on Thursday October 3rd and I had my baby the same night at 9- 45 P.M.

He weighed 8 lbs, has black hairy blue eyes and I Thank God he is a strong baby and is quiet so far.

Now that I have seen him I doubt if I will part with him, he would make life worth living. Hope I'll see you soon again.

yours Sincerely
Catherine C.

Euntes

the rain
sprung off
the hare

...

END

On Reflection

We drift in and out of people's lives.

Like water we are all currents in the same sea
Greens and Blues
Light, reflecting light

It is colourless without us.

. . .

Poems of the excerpts

and
four letters

Ripples

I have this thing I put on lips
Take it places whether it likes it or not
Tastes like red devils did
And everything strawberry should
In summers

Nothing massive happens really with it or not
Words still come and go regardless
Weather stays the same
Buses still don't smile splashing puddles

All things we carry stay with us
Whether we like it or not
Nothing that used to
Will taste as good as it did

But kisses are full of seasons
Ekmen, Friesens, Ellsworths
across the waves of minutiae

And over flower tops
they come like unexpected seasons
Catch our breath
Hold our mind

They are Summer, Rain, Regrets
Powerful as a butterfly

None more than you

I

My love for you are thoughts and wants

And memories of static looks that remain
Artforms in the corridor of my life where I have
seen you

Once I stood in the rain just to look at love in
your eyes
Then once in the sun
Both are equal
I feel the rain and love it
You make me love it

How it taps on my spine a cold pinch that this is
real

That I do feel
and it is you I see

And the Sun, the heat, the dust of summer
Looking at you
wanting you

Wanting to hold you when unsaid words build up
inside and muffle
and want to spend out all at once in a kiss

And your hips
how I watch them and how they stand
How shapely you are

And your hands
their squareness
their equalness
The little way you hold them
and how I want to hold them

Kiss them every chance I see them near

And how I pass you and touch you and want to
not pass

Your eyes when you are relaxed with me
how you love me back

How you see inside me and maybe see yourself

And your ways
and dress
that beg to me to flourish near you and your
scents

Ways that lure me unknowingly nearer
and make me want to rub against you
as horses do

Inhale you
Nibble you
And taste behind your ear

where I arouse myself against you
where words would fail again

I love you in myself and accept this
I feel this and keep it
Secret

It burns in me
fills me
weighs me

But I keep it

I want it
I want you
I want you

..

II

And I have stood in the wind and watched myself
in the glass
Blown and cold and loving you

I have said things and loaned you my heart
for times when I felt you could take it

And all of these things I have loved

None more than you
None more than you

And I have missed you
When I am starved of you I seek you
and refill the hall of my mind with your art

And I take from you
Always I take from you

I take your voice and expressions
the light coming off you as we stand by the
French doors
and I pretend pretence
Your touch when you are at ease next to me and
I fain indifference
though I swell with love for it

Your gentle playful slaps

Your food for me
I love your food for me

And my leaving
When I leave
I know it and it comes
and I leave

It has no value and I will give it none
I simply leave and know I will return
That I have stayed

That I have refilled on me
a perfume that will last until I do

And I am not lost to you
No
I am an equal with you
and so we are always whole
Even when apart

And that is good
That is good
That is a strength
And I love that too

And I thank you for trying
For saying you can be sorry to have missed me

And for thinking of me
And I know you have
But know not how
My thanks

And for time
Most of all for your time
My thanks

You are so generous with it
Very giving
My thanks

And your love
I have seen it
My Thanks

And your sensual being
always, always, always my thanks
And thoughts
And wants

Yes
I am guilty

But I am free

φ

four letters

⌘

four letters

They call me four letters in order
that the attentive stays until I die
like a milieu we weave
to soothe ourselves more than other mammals
yet not much more than money
such a trophic thing it is

And the trees we name must be so above us all
to stay in indignation and give us life
until we cut them on the quarter and rehearse
to remember men with names
thrown like random numbers at the noise
while we Quercus here and Cercis there
Water our palmatums
and sepia wood where Margo sits in Summer
now she's grown old
and the radio speaks of weather

And after we have filled the too-small table
with names of things we find content
we betray again the substance of aversion
and the stories come with place's names
that are wrong but we do not care –
anything but a silence

though Namaste is a silence
and still we name out sons our own
our daughters seasons, our perfumes feelings
neighbours Gods on fine days –
on wet days a decay

and we can only squinch our faces
when the heavens above us cry
because we do not get it
We do not understand at all

day one of New England's Fall
when the trees can take no more
and I – born in unmarried weave
am given four letters in order
that I turn when I am called and smile
near the village green
where Margo sits in Summer
where the oak trees cry
where my money can be taken
and numbers given
Least we forget

...

Thank you Amy.

You know who you are.

Love, S.

22814056R00101

Printed in Poland
by Amazon Fulfillment
Poland Sp. z o.o., Wrocław